Phonetic Groups in Chinese Characters: All Unrounded Vowel Finals in Mandarin Volume 4

by

Stephen M Kraemer

In looking at phonetic patterns of Chinese characters in Mandarin, many phonetic compound/phonetic element character pairs or groups exhibit certain final patterns. The phonetic patterns are based on the syllable structure of Modern Standard Mandarin, namely the syllable being composed of an initial, final, and tone. The final portion of the syllable is further composed of the rime (nuclear vowel + ending)(ending being a vowel or consonant).

One of the most interesting final patterns of Mandarin characters is the pattern of finals containing only unrounded vowels. These are pairs or groups of phonetic compound/phonetic element characters that exhibit any combination of the all unrounded vowel finals

"a" [a], "ai" [ai], "e" [ɤ], "ei" [ei], "ie" [iɛ], "ia" [ia], "i" [i], "i" [¹], "i" [ʅ]

(For vowel and consonant features in Mandarin, see Kratochvil 1968).

In this study, three groups of phonetic characters with all unrounded vowel finals in Mandarin will be shown. These include the 介 (jiè) group, where all characters share the common phonetic element 介 (jiè); the 皆 (jiē) group, where all characters share the common phonetic element 皆 (jiē); and the 切 (qiē, qiè) group, where all characters share the common phonetic element 切 (qiē, qiè).

Providing information about the phonetic patterns of Chinese characters and their corresponding phonetic elements may serve to help the student of Chinese to recognize the phonetic relationship among many characters in Mandarin. Teachers of Chinese may also find this book useful in seeing how phonetic elements can be arranged to show how they share certain features of their pronunciation with other characters. Character pronunciations are given in pinyin and are taken from Zhou You-guang (1980), based on Xin

Hua Zidian (1971). Where the phonetic element character pronunciation is not found in either Zhou You-guang (1980) or Xin Hua Zidian (1971), it is taken from Handian (2004 – 2015).

介 (jiè)

介 (jiè)

芥 (jiè)
蚧 (jiè)
界 (jiè)
疥 (jiè)
价 (jiè)

Phonetic Pattern:

Totally Perfect
(jiè)

芥 (jiè)

蚧 (jiè)

界 (jiè)

疥 (jiè)

价 (jiè)

介 (jiè)

阶 (jiē)
价 (jie)

Phonetic Pattern:

Segment Perfect
(jie)

阶 (jiē)
价 (jie)

介 (jiè)

价 (jià)

Phonetic Pattern:

Initial-Medial Perfect
(ji)
Palatal + i (jia, jie)
Unrounded Vowel Finals
(Diphthongs)
(ia, ie)
Tone Perfect (Tone 4)

价 (jià)

介 (jiè)

芥 (gài)

Phonetic Pattern:
Velar /Palatal
(g/j)
Velar + a (gai)
Palatal + i (jie)
Unrounded Vowel Finals
(Diphthongs)
(ai, ie)
Tone Perfect (Tone 4)
Similar Vowel
(i)
芥(gài)

介(jiè)

尬(gà)

Phonetic Pattern:

Velar /Palatal
(g/j)
Velar + a (ga)
Palatal + i (jie)
Unrounded Vowel Finals
(a, ie)
Tone Perfect (Tone 4)

尬(gà)

皆(jiē)

皆(jiē)

喈(jiē)
楷(jiē)

Phonetic Pattern:

Totally Perfect
(jiē)

喈(jiē)
楷(jiē)

皆 (jiē)

偕 (xié)
谐 (xié)

Phonetic Pattern:
Palatal
(x/j)

Final Perfect
(ie)

偕(xié)
谐(xié)

皆(jiē)

揩(kāi)

Phonetic Pattern:

Velar /Palatal
(k/j)
Velar + a (kai)
Palatal + i (jie)
Unrounded Vowel Finals
(Diphthongs)
(ai, ie)
Tone Perfect (Tone 1)
Similar Vowel
(i)
揩(kāi)

皆(jiē)

楷(kǎi)
锴(kǎi)

Phonetic Pattern:

Velar /Palatal

(k/j)

Velar + a (kai)

Palatal + i (jie)

Unrounded Vowel Finals

(Diphthongs)

(ai, ie)

Similar Vowel

(i)

楷(kǎi)

锴(kǎi)

切(qiē, qiè)

切(qiè)

窃(qiè)

Phonetic Pattern:

Totally Perfect
(qiè)

窃 (qiè)

切(qiē)

窃(qiè)

Phonetic Pattern:

Segment Perfect
(qie)

窃(qiè)

切(qiē)

沏(qī)

Phonetic Pattern:
Initial Perfect
(q)
Palatal + i (qi, qie)
Unrounded Vowel Finals
(i, ie)
Tone Perfect (Tone 1)
Similar Vowel
(i)

沏(qī)

切(qiē)

砌(qì)

Phonetic Pattern:
Initial Perfect
(q)
Palatal + i (qi, qie)
Unrounded Vowel Finals
(i, ie)
Similar Vowel
(i)

砌(qì)

切(qiè)

砌(qì)

Phonetic Pattern:

Initial Perfect
(q)
Palatal + i (qi, qie)
Unrounded Vowel Finals
(i, ie)
Tone Perfect (Tone 4)
Similar Vowel
(i)

砌 (qì)

切(qiè)

沏(qī)

Phonetic Pattern:
Initial Perfect
(q)
Palatal + i (qi, qie)
Unrounded Vowel Finals
(i, ie)
Similar Vowel
(i)

沏 (qī)

切(qiè)

彻(chè)

Phonetic Pattern:

Retroflex/Palatal
(ch/q)
Retroflex + e (che)
Palatal + i (qie)
Unrounded Vowel Finals
(e, ie)
Tone Perfect (Tone 4)
Similar Vowel
(e)
彻(chè)

切(qiē)

彻(chè)

Phonetic Pattern:
Retroflex/Palatal
(ch/q)
Retroflex + e (che)
Palatal + i (qie)
Unrounded Vowel Finals
(e, ie)
Similar Vowel
(e)

彻(chè)

References

Cheng, C.C. (1973). *A synchronic phonology of Mandarin Chinese.* The Hague: Mouton.

Handian [<汉典>, '字典']. Online Chinese dictionary. (2004 – 2015). http://www.zdic.net

Kraemer, Stephen M. (1980). *Potentially pedagogically useful phonetics in the Chinese script: Their identification and characterization.* Doctoral dissertation. Rutgers University.

Kraemer, Stephen M. (1991a). *Sound clues in Mandarin character phonetic series.* Retrieved from https://scholarsbank.uoregon.edu/xmlui/handle/1794/4943

Kraemer, Stephen M. (1991b). *Levels of phonological regularity in the Chinese writing system.* Retrieved from https://scholarsbank.uoregon.edu/xmlui/handle/1794/8133

Kraemer, Stephen M. (2017). *Let's Learn Mandarin Phonics.* CreateSpace Independent Publishing Platform.

Kraemer, Stephen M. (2017). *Let's Learn Mandarin Phonics-2.* CreateSpace Independent Publishing Platform.

Kraemer, Stephen M. (2018a). *Let's Learn Mandarin Phonics-3. Rime Clue, Rime-Tone Clue, Ending Clue, Ending-Tone Clue Phonetic Patterns of Common Chinese Characters.* CreateSpace Independent Publishing Platform.

Kraemer, Stephen M. (2018b). *Let's Learn Mandarin Phonics-4. Initial Clue, Initial-Tone Clue, Tone-Clue and Related Phonetic Patterns of Common Chinese Characters.* CreateSpace Independent Publishing Platform.

Kraemer, Stephen M. (2018c). *Let's Learn Mandarin Phonics-5. Vowel Phonetic Clues for Common Chinese Characters.* CreateSpace Independent Publishing Platform.

Kraemer, Stephen M. (2018d). *Phonetic Clues for Learning Common Chinese Characters.* CreateSpace Independent Publishing Platform.

Kraemer, Stephen M. (2018e). *A Phonetic Guide to Learning Chinese Characters.* CreateSpace Independent Publishing Platform.

Kraemer, Stephen M.(2020). *Phonetic Patterns in Mandarin Chinese Characters: Pinyin "ng" Ending Finals with Unrounded Vowels*. Independent Publishing Platform.

Kraemer, Stephen M.(2020a). *Phonetic Patterns in Mandarin Chinese Characters: Pinyin "n/ng" Ending Finals with Unrounded Vowels*. Independent Publishing Platform.

Kraemer, Stephen M.(2020b). *Phonetic Patterns in Mandarin Chinese Characters: V/VC1 Finals.* Independent Publishing Platform.

Kraemer, Stephen M.(2020c). *Phonetic Patterns in Mandarin Chinese Characters: VC1 Finals with Unrounded Vowels.* Independent Publishing Platform.

Kraemer, Stephen M.(2020d). *Phonetic Patterns in Mandarin Chinese Characters: V Finals with a Rounded Medial Vowel Plus Unrounded V.* Independent Publishing Platform.

Kraemer, Stephen M.(2020e). *Phonetic Patterns in Mandarin Chinese Characters: V Finals with a Rounded Ending Vowel Plus Unrounded V.* Independent Publishing Platform.

Kraemer, Stephen M.(2020f). *Phonetic Patterns in Mandarin Chinese Characters: Labial/Velar Initials and Pinyin "m"/"w"*. Independent Publishing Platform.

Kraemer, Stephen M.(2020g). *Phonetic Patterns in Mandarin Chinese Characters: Velar/Retroflex Initials*. Independent Publishing Platform.

Kraemer, Stephen M.(2020h). *Phonetic Patterns in Mandarin Chinese Characters: Velar/Alveolar Initials.* Independent Publishing Platform.

Kraemer, Stephen M.(2020i). *Phonetic Patterns in Mandarin Chinese Characters: Palatal Initials.* Independent Publishing Platform.

Kraemer, Stephen M.(2020j). *Phonetic Patterns in Chinese Characters: Pinyin "a/e" Variation in Mandarin.* Independent Publishing Platform.

Kraemer, Stephen M.(2020k). *Phonetic Groups in Chinese Characters: All Unrounded Vowel Finals in Mandarin.* Independent Publishing Platform.

Kraemer, Stephen M.(2020l). *Phonetic Groups in Chinese Characters: All Unrounded Vowel Finals in Mandarin Volume 2.* Independent Publishing Platform.

Kraemer, Stephen M.(2020m). *Phonetic Groups in Chinese Characters: All Unrounded Vowel Finals in Mandarin Volume 3.* Independent Publishing Platform.

Kraemer, Stephen M.(2020n). *Phonetic Groups in Chinese Characters: All Vowel Finals in Mandarin*. Independent Publishing Platform.

Kraemer, Stephen M.(2020o). *Phonetic Groups in Chinese Characters: All Vowel Finals in Mandarin Volume 2*. Independent Publishing Platform.

Kraemer, Stephen M.(2020p). *Phonetic Groups in Chinese Characters: All Vowel Finals in Mandarin Volume 3.* Independent Publishing Platform.

Kraemer, Stephen M.(2020q). *Phonetic Patterns in Mandarin Chinese Characters: Final Perfect with Palatal j/x, q/x Initials.* Independent Publishing Platform.

Kratochvil, Paul. (1968). *The Chinese language today: Features of an emerging standard*. London: Hutchinson & Co., Ltd.

Xinhua zidian (New China dictionary). (1971). Beijing: Shangwu Yinshuguan. [<新华字典>, 1971, 北京: 商务印书馆.

Zhou, Youguang. (1980). *Hanzi shengpang duyin biancha* (A handy look up for the pronunciation of phonetics in Chinese characters). Jilin: Jilin Remnin Chubanshe.
[周 有光, 1980, <汉字声旁读音便查>, 吉林: 吉林人民出版社.]